EXPERIENCING A FAITH FULGOD

Holding on to the faithfulness of God in the face of uncertainty, discouragement, and doubt.

Gladys Onoh

Copyright

ISBN: 978-1-7362183-4-1 (Paperback)
ISBN: 978-1-7362183-3-4 (Ebook)

Library of Congress Control Number: 9781736218341

Cover Design by Emmanuella Ben-eboh
Edited by Winifred Obanor
Layout by Kingdom Branding

Printed in the United States of America

This book is dedicated to you. As you go through the journey of having a better experience of God's faithfulness, may your light shine brighter, may your life become richer and your courage stronger

About the Book

This book was birthed in the place of encounter with the Holy Spirit; through obedience to God's instructions, His words have become flesh. This book is for everyone, no matter what season of life you find yourself in. It will especially help those dealing with doubt and serve as encouragement for those needing a reminder of God's faithfulness. Perhaps you are in the stage of your life where you feel disconnected from God or wonder if He is listening to you, this book will equip you with the scriptures for edification and direction that you need.

What to Expect

By the end of this book, you will have the confidence to handle life's season and a better knowing that God is backing you. You will be armed with the right tools to lead life with the boldness that Christ gives in His Word. Your thought patterns, especially about God, will transition you into having a more tangible experience with God. My prayer for you is that you will have a deeper understanding about God and His immeasurable love for you. So, get excited and expectant as you dive into the book—**How to Experience the Faithfulness of Our God.**

Table of Contents

STANDING ON A FAITHFUL TRUTH

We know some core things as believers. By 'believers,' I meanpeople who have accepted Jesus Christ as their Lord, Savior, and Guardian – and who have a working relationship with Him. In case you do not know what, those core things are, here's a refresher:

One

The Word of God is true. It can never change. It is there to help us, encourage us, and direct us in living our lives with purpose, joy, satisfaction, and fulfillment. Get this: the word of the Lord is faithful to manifest in every situation of our lives no matter how dire or hopeless it may look. The Word of God is the truth that never fails, and you can confidently count on it.

Two

God cannot be against you. However, there are instances where situations might prove contrary. In those situations, God might not be pleased with what you are doing or what you have done. There is a difference—God is for you, and so He can express displeasure and reproof when you are acting contrary to His plan and will for you. In the instance you recognize your actions have gone in a direction that does not stand well with God, you should reconcile with Him. God loves you too much to hold things against you, and He wants you to know love more than anything else. When you know and begin to comprehend the depth of God's love, you have a better understanding of how to relate with Him. Remember, God corrects those He loves (Heb 12:6), so it is a blessing to receive correction from God.

Three

Guilt is not from God. Let me repeat this because we need to understand it very well so that the enemy does not use it against us: feeling and dwelling in guilt is not of God. Yes, the Holy Spirit can convict you in an attempt to realign you in God's path. However, the purpose of the conviction is to urge you to make corrections, not to guilt you or trap you in your wrongs. God is faithful to forgive.

When He forgives you, the wrongs stay forgiven and forgotten. This means that you can bask in God's mercy where there is no regret.

Action Step

Throughout your day today, be conscious of God's faithfulness. Meditate on the bible verses for today's devotional and be intentional about standing on God's truth.

Prayer

My faithful God and father help me to remember your faithfulness, to have trust in your unfailing words, and live out my purpose in your glory.

Zephaniah 3:17 ESV / *The Lord your God is in your midst, a mighty one who will save; he will rejoice over you with gladness; he will quiet you by his love; he will exult over you with loud singing.*

1 John 1:9 ESV / *If we confess our sins, he is faithful and just to forgive us our sins and to cleanse us from all unrighteousness.*

Isaiah 46:10 / *I declare from the beginning how it will end and foretell from the start what has not yet happened. I decree that my purpose will stand, and I will fulfill my every plan.*

FAITHFUL TO CARE

There are times when you find yourself in situations that make you question if God cares for you at all. I know that I have been there before. I am happy to say having that experience helped me not only to realize God's care for me, but it is also helping me to encourage others who doubt God's care. I have also seen people who questioned if God cared for them due to the magnitude of their circumstances. I am not sure if you are familiar with the story of Naomi, a Hebrew woman in the Old Testament who lost everything including her wealth, husband, and children (Ruth 1:120). She was very certain that God did not care about her, and even went ahead to change her name to Mara—to signify the bitterness she felt. She tried to distant herself from other people so she could wallow alone in her sorrow.

However, something strange happened. There was someone who will not allow Naomi to be alone and that was Naomi's son's widow, Ruth.

She refused to desert Naomi no matter how much Naomi tried to push Ruth away. Ruth stuck with Naomi every step of the way, even when Naomi returned to her hometown. Ruth took the risk of going to a land she has never been to before and a place where she is not even accepted due to her status as a Moabite. I want to tell you that Ruth was a physical manifestation of God's care for Naomi. When Naomi thought there was no one else on earth who was her family or who cared for her, God used Ruth to remind her that she was not alone.

Do you know that no matter how much we might try to deny it, there is a FAITHFUL FACT? The fact is the truth of God: we are never alone. God is always with us and will always be with us. He can use someone, something, a sign, a word, or even use someone's kindness to remind us that He is with us. God cares for you, and He will always put you before first. Do not let unanswered prayer, financial burdens, lack of fruitfulness, stress, or overwhelming life circumstances make you forget about His care. Sometimes, we can be too overwhelmed with our problems to see that God is caring. Like in Naomi's story, God used Ruth to keep her company, console her, and even give her grandchildren which she did not have before. When Naomi took her eyes off her bitter situation and focused on making sure that Ruth was very well settled, she benefited from her relationship with Ruth and she began to experience joy again. I want to challenge you to take your eyes off your bitter situation and focus on God's care.

Action Step

How to concentrate on God's care:

1. Remember all the times that God has shown up for you
2. Remember He used an individual to help you or lessen a burden
3. Do you reconcile with God when you thought there was no way out but suddenly God showed you a way?
4. Journal your care experience with God
5. Appreciate Him for caring
6. Let Him know that you are faithful in His care for you

Prayer

My hope is faithful in You because I know that Your Word says You are for me and You care for me. I am thankful because You never leave me alone. I have confidence that You will always do what is best for me.

Isaiah 14:24 ESV / *The Lord of hosts has sworn: "As I have planned, so shall it be, and as I have purposed, so shall it stand,*

Isaiah 41:13 NLT / *for I hold you by your right hand, I the Lord your God. And I say to you, 'Don't be afraid. I am here to help you.*

TOO FAITHFUL TOBE DISCOURAGED

Discouragement is common, and sometimes even the strongest person feels discouraged. Discouragement can be stirred up in different ways. You may feel it when someone is insensitively offering you unsolicited advice, when you notice things that others may have that you do not have, or when you are comparing your timeline to your expectations of what should have happened by now. Once discouragement creeps into your mind, it can be hard to get it out. It can make you question your faith and deflate your hope. The scripture I am reminded of whenever I feel discouraged is that in Matthew 15:11. In that scripture, Jesus tells his disciples, "it is not what goes into someone's mouth that defiles them; it is what comes out of the mouth that defiles them." Every single day, you see things that have the potential to discourage you from your walk with God or boost your faith. It may be something that discourages you from having hope or someone that makes you feel discouraged. The truth is avoidance cannot always be the answer. You must learn to make sure that no matter how many discouraging things you see around you, what comes out of you must be different and bolster your faith walk. Just like Jesus said to His disciples then, He is saying it to us now. It is what comes out of you that matters because it originates and speaks of deep-seated belief systems in the heart. So be faithful to yourself and make sure no matter how discouraged you might feel, do not house this feeling in your heart.

Also, understand that although timelines are important, timelines on your goals are not deadlines for God. Your timeline is not a way to tell God that He must act by or before a certain time. Your timeline is for you. It is a way of holding yourself accountable. A timeline provides a way for you to measure where you are, how you are going to get to where you want to be, and what you need to do to get there. If we are not careful, we set our timelines as a due date for God to act and get frustrated when our expectations are not fulfilled. God's attribute is beyond us and deeper than what we can understand. One of His attributes is having structures and processes in place. Although it is hard to admit, I have been in a situation where I tried to manipulate the timing of God. I tried forcing things severely, and I ended up frustrated and disappointed. I have been intentional in learning to trust God's process and timing because I know that He is too faithful, and he has notforgotten His promises to me.

Be encouraged by God's faithfulness, His ability and love for you. Do not give room for discouragement don't run with the mindset that says, "it is easier said than done" rather switch up your mindset with this mantra "it gets easier the more I do it.'' Being intentional about what comes out of you will help you curb discouragement. Surrender your heart to the Holy Spirit and submit your expectations to God. God can never give you a snake when you ask for fish; neither will He give you a scorpion when you ask for an egg. He is working to perfect your expectations and answer your prayers beyond your imaginations.

When you feel discouraged, I challenge you to encourage someone who you know is going through a difficult time. You can even pray for them according to the leading of the Holy Spirit. As you do so, you are proving to discouragement that you have no time to wallow in this feeling because you have business to take care of. When you encourage someone else while you feel discouraged, you not only experience the strength of the Holy Spirit, but you sow a seed that God will honor. Galatian 6:6 reminds us that God cannot be mocked. Whatever a man sows, he will reap in return; so, as you sow encouragement or prayers to others, God gives you a harvest of encouragement and prayers as well. Since God is the one giving the reward, then you have nothing to worry about. God always gives a bountiful reward.

Action Step

Remember that avoidance will not always solve the problem of discouragement. Commit to yourself by making sure that you do not allow discouragement to take root in your heart.

Prayer

Holy Spirit help me to be intentional about what comes out of my heart. I close every door that I have opened for discouragement to creep in. I stand in God's faithfulness to decree that my courage is renewed, and my hope is alive.

Matthew 15:11 NIV / *where Jesus was telling his disciples "What goes into someone's mouth does not defile them, but what comes out of their mouth, that is what defiles them."*

Luke 11:11-12 NIV / *What father among you, if his son asks for a fish,* *will give him a snake instead of a fish? Or if they ask for an egg, do you give them a scorpion? Of course not!*

Galatian 6:6-7 BSB / *But the one who receives instruction in the word must share in all good things with his instructor. Do not be deceived: God cannot be mocked. Whatever a man sows, he will reap in return.*

MY RESPONSE TO A FAITHFUL GOD

Do you know that God watches to see how we respond to Him,how we respond to our situations, and how we respond to others about God? The way you respond to God is critical because it reflects the condition of your heart. When you are faced with challenges, your response determines how the journey through that challenge will be. So, remember this the next time you are faced with something you do not like. In today's reading, I will show you the ways you should respond to God; the way you should respond to your situation, and the ways you should respond to others about God.

Responding to God

Let God know that you have trust in Him. Sometimes, you feel that you have trust in God but then your faith may waver. Though this is not ideal, it is normal. Don't beat yourself up about it, just do your best to get back on track. Secondly, God needs to know that you have faith in His abilities to turn situations around. He needs to know that you believe in the possibilities of what He can do for you. He needs to know that you completely have faith and trust that He will do it. When you have these attitudes towards God, or when you respond confident as someone who knows God's authority, He takes responsibility for you. He is a God that takes responsibility for His children and for His actions. He is not irresponsible; He is a faithful God. I challenge you today to boast about God. You must have confidence in God that He will do what He has promised to do. Your confidence in God causes Him to move swiftly for you because He is moved by faith. He can NEVER leave you hanging.

Responding to Your Situation

Do you know that your situation will be as scary as you are powerful? And it will also be as powerful as you are fearful. Let me explain to you what I mean by this. Imagine a scenario where one is dealing with sickness (this could apply to any of life's challenges). The way you respond to the sickness will tell the sickness who the boss is. You know that every awful thing that happens is not of God (see James 1:13). Some challenges come to deter you from God and cause you to lose faith. Knowing this, you must respond to difficult situations with the confidence that Jesus Christ used in defeating death and conquering darkness. You must respond with the confidence that says, "I know whose I am therefore I know what my life and my body can and cannot accommodate (Psalm 82:6). This is the Christ confidence that declares that there is no accommodation for sickness in my body. There is only room for light in my life. There is no accommodation for foolishness and foolish decisions because I have endured with the wisdom of God that surpasses human understanding. I am God's extension, so my body cannot accommodate any kind of illness. I am God's own so my life cannot be a dwelling place for poverty. I am God's child therefore I cannot be timid where I am supposed to be bold. I am God's reflection so I cannot live or lead a life that is below God. You have to declare it, you must pray it, you must think about it, and you must speak it. The time is now to show the challenges in your life that you are a no-nonsense believer of God's power. Therefore, respond to your situation correctly.

Responding to Others AboutGod in You Situation

People are watching when you are going through a tough time or when you are having a pleasant time. Let your response to people be consistent no matter what season they catch you in. Do not let people project their fears on you.

Do not let them make you feel terrible for not worrying and, most importantly, do not let anyone belittle your faith in God.

Respond to people in faith, not in agreement with the negativity. For instance, someone might say to you, “You are getting old. When you will have your babies?” You respond, “Don’t worry about me because my God is faithful and does great things. My babies are coming.” They may say, “You are getting older, but you are not married.” You respond, “Please do not be afraid on my behalf because I will be married. My faithful God is writing my love story.” They say, “You had a child out of wedlock, so you should not have high expectations when it comes to marriage. You should just settle.” You respond, “My expectations will not be cut short because my God can fulfill my expectations.” The moment you begin to sympathize with people who are concerned or worried for you, that is the moment you start to waver in your faith. You do not need anyone to project their pressure, their fear, their disappointment onto you. You need to respond to people boldly in faith.

Action Step

How have you responded previously to your faithful God? Start today to make conscious efforts to respond in ways that show God’s faithfulness.

Prayer

God, please help me to accurately respond to you, to my situation, and to people around me in ways that please you and brings your glory and pleasure.

Hebrews 10:23 ESV / *"Let us hold fast the confession of our hope without wavering, for he who promised is faithful."*

Proverb 23:18 NLT / *There is surely a future hope for you, and your hope will not be cut off.*

Jeremiah 9:24 NIV / *but let him who boasts boast of this, that he understands and knows Me, that I am the Lord who exercises lovingkindness, justice and righteousness on earth; for I delight in these things," declares the Lord.*

FAITHFUL TO GROW

You must be familiar with the saying, "getting older is inevitable, but growth and maturity are intentional." This phrase is applicable as believers in our walk with Christ. Being a progressive believer requires you to be a growing believer; someone who is constantly in the space to increase maturity as you work towards being like our role model, Jesus Christ. You have to be faithful in your Christian growth. Being faithful in your growth requires you to know how to conduct yourself amidst crisis, confusion, or criticism. Many of us typically do well in our faith as long as we do not experience anything that shakes our growth. Being faithful to growth means allowing God to see how seriously you take Him and letting people around you see the transitions and transformation in your life. Growing means leaving behind things that do not encourage your growth. This means deliberately picking things, people, activities, environments that challenge you to be a better version of yourself.

One thing that could encourage growth in your faith is knowing how to consciously respond and handle hurt, betrayal, or unhealthy and ungodly competitions. Being faithful in your growth means that you are not swayed by popular or ungodly trends. It means that you are not conforming to ways that displease God. The Bible says that "the blessings of the Lord are upon the man who does not go in the direction of wicked people; the man who does not stand in the way of sinners or sit in the company of mockers." (Psalm 1:1 NIV)

As a believer, you are destined to do great things. Perhaps you may not have realized it, or you may not understand it, or you may not even know it. God, who is all-knowing, knows the path to your destiny. This is why sometimes you might find that the Holy Spirit stops you from making decisions that could ruin you. I remember when the phase YOLO (You Only Live Once) was trending. I was feeling it. Of course, I wanted to use YOLO as an excuse to make stupid choices. I finally thought this was my year to let loose and live on the edge. I remember going to an event and my goal for that day was to get drunk and have fun like never before. Well, I tasted one drink and I hated it. I only took one sip and I started feeling strange. I thought to myself, "Why? Why is it always that my "fun story" will end differently than expected?" However, I did not realize then that God was protecting me from making a terrible mistake. A few weeks later, I lost a close friend who died of alcohol poisoning.

YOLO is not "bad" because, the truth is, you do only live once. But what kind of life do you want to live? If you want to use YOLO as an excuse for something, it should be your motivation to make this one life count, to lead a life that shows the faithfulness of God, and to live a life that can inspire others to know and love God. To lead a life that promotes Jesus Christ, a life that when people look at you, they give glory to God because you are changing lives.

Being faithful to grow is realizing that there is much required of you so you must intentionally work towards being all that you are ordained to be. It requires you to realize that the more you grow and mature, the more you might have to let people go. The more you will have to let go of the idea of everyone liking you. The more you will have to realize that although you are sent, you are not sent to everyone. Faithfulness in your growth process will require you to lose holds of things, ideas, or even environments that do not contribute to that growth. Growth requires faithfulness from your part to commit to whatever that growth could mean to you per season. It requires trust in God to lead you through different parts of your growth process. Growth means giving honor and respect to whom it is due and understanding that you cannot respect anybody enough to violate your conscience. Growth means you do not respect anybody so much that you ignore your spiritual sensitivity. You should not respect anybody enough to discard your sensitivity to growth.

Action Step

What are some things currently distracting you from your growth? In what areas are you sensing that God wants you to grow? I challenge you to take positive actions towards your growth.

Prayer

Dear Lord, thank you for growth. I am grateful for the processes that you are taking me through to help me become all that you have ordained me to be. Father, I ask that you help me stay consistent, faithful, and committed to my growth. Let all stages of my life bring you glory in Jesus name, Amen.

Psalm 1:1 NIV / *Blessed is the man who does not walk in the counsel of the wicked or stand in the way of sinners or sit in the seat of mockers. But his delight is in the law of the LORD, and on his law, he meditates day and night.*

1 Timothy 4:15 / *Be diligent in these matters; give yourself wholly to them, so that everyone may see your progress.*

1 Corinthians 13:11 / *When I was a child, I talked like a child, I thought* *like a child, I reasoned like a child. When I became a man, I put the ways of childhood behind me.*

FAITHFUL TO FULFILL

Our God does not go back on His promises. The Bible says thatHis covenants are sure. When He says He will do something, you have to be to rest assured that He will do it. Most of the time, in our waiting seasons, the end looks so far, and the manifestations so unattainable. But I have come to realize that, as a Christian, things will always work out for your good. It is only a matter of time. One of the stories from scripture that encourages me is the story of Jabez in 1 Chronicles 4:9-10. The Bible said in 1 Chronicles 4:9 "Now Jabez was more honorable than his brothers, and his mother called his name Jabez, meaning "I bore him in pain." It makes me wonder how someone who was considered to be more honorable, more distinguished, and nobler than his brothers yet had such an unfortunate situation surrounding him. Jabez's name did not speak to his character of being honorable.

His name spoke against everything good that he stood for. His name meant pain: the one born out of pain. God is too faithful not to fulfill our requests. When you pray, when you cry, when you ask, be encouraged to know that God has heard you and He will fulfill your request. You see, Jabez saw that the circumstances surrounding his life didn't seem pleasant. He took action to change it. Jabez appealed to God to change his life.

> *And Jabez called on the God of Israel saying, "Oh, that You would bless me indeed, and enlarge my territory, that Your hand would be with me, and that You would keep me from evil, that I may not cause pain!" So, God granted him what he requested." (1 Chronicles 4:9-10).*

I know that I am not the only one who can relate to Jabez's story. A story with a painful, terrible, stigmatized past, and almost a hopeless future. No matter what stage of life you are in, Jabez's story can be relatable to you in one way or the other. The takeaway I want you to have out of Jabez's story is the victory that he experienced. He prayed to a faithful God and that God turned his life around. God granted Jabez his request and He will grant you your request as well. God wants to do great things in and through you. He has the ability to do what He said He would do. When you are faced with discouragement,

I challenge you to remind yourself that my God can do what He said He would do. Do you know that the word faithful is synonymous with devoted, loyal, trustworthy, steadfast, constant, precise, and accurate? Just think about it for a second and try to pair God's characteristics with any of the words I mentioned above. You will notice that they fit perfectly. Our God is all that and more. Truthfully, He is ready to show us all that He is. He is a faithful God who fulfills. Be constantly reminded of that and trust in it.

Action Step

God is faithful to fulfill. It does not matter how many times you need to remind yourself of this fact as long as you don't forget it. Be rest assured and rest on His faithfulness.

Prayer

My dear Lord, I am confident in your ability to bring to manifest everything that you have promised me. Help my heart not to waver. Thank you because I know that, just like Jabez, you will grant me my requests in Jesus' name, Amen.

1 Chronicles 4:9-10 / *And Jabez called on the God of Israel saying, "Oh, that You would bless me indeed, and enlarge my territory, that Your hand would be with me, and that You would keep me from evil, that I may not cause pain!" So, God granted him what he requested."*

Ezekiel 12:28 ESV / *Therefore say to them, thus says the Lord God: None of my words will be delayed any longer, but the word that I speak will be performed, declares the Lord God."*

TOO FAITHFUL TO BE DOUBTED

Tell me one person that God promised to do something for and never fulfilled it? Whether it is in the Bible or people you know, God has a track record of keeping His Word. The Bible said that every good and perfect gift comes from the Lord James1:17). Every bad or not so perfect gift does not come from God. As human beings, we deal with doubts. And one of my personal favorites scripture to hold on to is - is every word from His mouth fulfills what He intends and does not fall to the ground (Isaiah 55:11). We can get discouraged and many times even get disappointed at God, but do you know that those are not the attributes of God? I could bet you that God has shown you faithfulness in areas of your life that you might not even recognize. Many things cause us to doubt ourselves or to doubt others, in some extreme cases, we may even doubt God, but do you know that disappointment, unreliability, untrustworthiness are not the attributes or characteristics associated with God?

The Bible said in Proverbs 13:12 that "hope deferred makes the heart sick, but a longing fulfilled is a tree of life". When expectations fail, of course, it makes it harder to believe again, but I heard someone say that good things come to those who wait, and miracles happen to those that don't give up. There are many instances in the Bible where people who doubted God experienced His faithfulness. These instances are there as a sounding board and as a reminder for us to believe. One of the popular cases that we are very familiar with is the story of Sarah in the book of Genesis. When the angel of the Lord told Sarah that she was going to have a baby, it was very easy for Sarah to doubt it. To be frank, I feel like anyone in her shoes would have doubted it as well, but Sarah did not know that she was about to experience God in a way that she had never experienced before. She was about to have a God experience that several generations after her would talk about. Women and men on earth were going to use her story as an encouragement to believe when believing feels impossible. Although Sarah was an older woman with potential reproductive difficulties, what God told her didn't look like what she knew. It looked like it went against everything in her life. God showed Sarah that His words are not to be doubted, because He is faithful in action.

If there are many things that we doubt— the ability, authority, and strength of God to do what He has promised should not be one of them. Doubt was displayed in the book of Matthew 14:28-31, where the disciples saw Jesus walking on water and were baffled. Peter being so bold called out to Jesus and asked Jesus that if He truly is the one, He should beckon Peter to walk with Him on the water. Jesus accepted Peter's challenge and asked him to join Him on top of the water. Amazing, right?

So, Peter stepped out of the boat and started walking towards Jesus Christ on the water. But guess what? Suddenly, Peter began sinking into the water. I believe that Peter began to sink because he was afraid and took his eyes of Christ. You know you can be afraid, but I dare you not to take your eyes off Jesus Christ. Taking your eyes off Christ shows your doubt and I will prove it to you. In the same verse, Matthew 14:31, the Bible states that as Peter began to sink, he cried out, "Lord, save me!" Immediately, Jesus reached out His hand and caught him. "You of little faith," Jesus said to Peter, "why did you doubt?" So, you see, before Peter even became afraid, he had doubts in his mind. Doubt distorts your image of God's promises. The objective of doubt is to make you feel uncertain and insecure, but your objective is to make sure that you fix your eyes on Jesus and on His faithfulness.

Even when you are afraid, don't take your eyes off God. Rather submit your feelings of fear and doubt to Him and watch God move for you.

Action Step

In what way have doubts distorted your vision, goals, relationships, or your trust in God? Challenge those areas with the word of God.

Prayer

In Jesus' name, I stand against every spirit of fear in my life, I take charge of my life, I speak and believe that's no room for doubts in my life in Jesus name, Amen!!

Matthew 14:22-31 / *Immediately Jesus made the disciples get into the boat and go on ahead of him to the other side, while he dismissed the crowd. After he had dismissed them, he went up on a mountainside by himself to pray. Later that night, he was there alone, and the boat was already a considerable distance from land, buffeted by the waves because the wind was against it. Shortly before dawn, Jesus went out to them, walking on the lake. \ When the disciples saw him walking on the lake, they were terrified. "It's a ghost," they said and cried out in fear. But Jesus* *immediately said to them: "Take courage! It is I. Don't be afraid." "Lord, if it's you," Peter replied, "tell me to come to you on the water. "Come," he said. Then Peter got down out of the boat, walked on the water, and came toward Jesus. 30 But when he saw the wind, he was afraid and, beginning to sink, cried out, "Lord, save me!" Immediately Jesus reached out his hand and caught him. "You of little faith," he said, "why did you doubt?"*

YOUR FAITHFULNESS TO YOURSELF

Our God is faithful even when we are not faithful. His faithfulness is not determined by our faithfulness. Although, some cases, show correlations between someone who is faithful and the abundance of God's faithfulness in that individual's life. However,the characteristic of God is not what you need to work for to see His faithfulness, nor do you have to give anything in exchange for His faithfulness. God is faithful and that's incontestable.

But listen, you owe yourself a faithfulness that no one else can give you. I once read somewhere that result is sweeter when you put in the work. Faithfulness to yourself is work that you must commit to. The difference between those who achieve their daily objectives, monthly goals, or yearly goals is their commitment to their goal and staying faithful to their course.

In the system of life, nothing can be given to someone who is not faithful. A time-sensitive job or task that might lead to promotion can't be entrusted to you because you haven't delivered before or have not passed previous faithfulness tests from God. God can't even trust an unfaithful child with something important. I remember hearing my Pastor say something that changed me. He said, "God cannot entrust His faithful son or daughter as a spouse to someone who is unfaithful and unreliable."

Faithfulness to yourself is not something that someone else can give to you, especially regarding your goals. Lack of faithfulness to yourself can be due to lack of motivation, procrastination, tiredness, stress, laziness and the likes. But can you overcome these? Absolutely! For instance, you will not always feel motivated to work towards your tasks or goals. Once you are reliant one day because you feel motivated, you will be reliant the next day, and you might even have a good excuse for it.

The solution to laziness, excuses, procrastination, lack of motivation is WILL POWER. Your will to achieve your goals and how badly you want them will keep you on track to accomplishing your goals. So, do you want it bad enough? The solution to stress and tiredness is getting needed the rest, sleep, and doing things that will refresh and refuel you. Fortunately, faithfulness is a learned skill that can be improved upon.

I challenge you today to be faithful. Stay committed and improve the areas of your life that are important to you. These can include the company you are presently working for, your family, your friendships, your life goals, and service in the kingdom of God.

Action Step

What are some of the things that have caused you to be faithful to yourself and to your goals and aspirations? I bet you that sometimes when you are being unfaithful, you know it. Moving forward, when you realize that you are slacking or being complacent, take action and quickly redirect yourself to being faithful.

Prayer

In the name of Jesus, I ask you Heavenly Father, to help me stay faithful. Endue me with the strength to be faithful and committed to everything that I have been called to do. I receive help from the Holy Spirit to function faithfully in Jesus name, Amen.

James 1:12 / *Blessed is the man who remains steadfast under trial, for when he has stood the test, he will receive the crown of life, which God haspromised to those who love him.*

Proverbs 13:4 / *The soul of the sluggard craves and gets nothing, while the soul of the diligent is richly supplied.*

Galatians 6:9 / *And let us not grow weary of doing good, for in due season we will reap, if we do not give up.*

Proverbs 28:20 / *"A faithful man will abound with blessings."*

Luke 16:12 / *"If you have not been faithful in what is another man's, who will give you what is your own?"*

TOO FAITHFUL TO ABANDON ME

Growing up as a teenager, I dealt with lots of abandonment issues. I didn't know that the root of what I was dealing with was abandonment until years later when I saw fruits of that seed.

During those years of dealing with abandonment, my friendships and my ability to accept new people and opportunities suffered. This struggle spilled over into my relationship with God and made it to suffer. When you are fighting with people, at least you can run to God and find counsel, but when you are fighting with God who do you run to? This was my situation. I didn't trust the love God had for me. I didn't think that God could be faithful to me because I knew that I wasn't faithful to God per se.

Every time I sinned or did anything that didn't please God, I thought that He was going to abandon me just like the people in my life. I thought God's faithfulness was something that I needed to work for. Well, you can imagine how that turned out. I was always in a rat race of righteousness and guilt. You know that we as humans cannot be righteous by ourselves. Our righteousness is in Christ who sacrificed and exchanged His precious life for us (1 Corinthians 1:30). Throughout this period of my life, God showed me His faithfulness. He taught me that I needed to trust in His love for me and that would eventually deliver me from myself, from my struggle with guilt, from my abandonment issues, and my doubt of God's faithfulness.

When you go through many phases in your life, be it dark periods, confusion, uncertainty of not knowing where you stand with God - listen, God will ALWAYS know where He stands with you. He will never leave you or forsake you, that is His promises to you (Deuteronomy 31:6). He stands right next to you, wrapping His arms around you. There's never a moment when God is not with you. The devil will make you think that God can disappoint you. Satan will make you think that God can and will abandon you. The enemy will even go as far as making you think that you are undeserving of God's faithfulness. Do not fall for these lies.

One of the scriptures that blesses me is Isaiah 43:2, where the Bible says, "When you pass through the waters, I will be with you; and through the rivers, they shall not overwhelm you; when you walk through fire you shall not be burned, and the flame shall not consume you because God is always there with you." God is always faithful and too faithful to ever abandon you. It is not in His character to be unfaithful, always remember that!

Action Step

Whenever the enemy tries to dissuade you from God's faithfulness, say out loud that God is too faithful to abandon me. Let this be your anchor because that's the truth of God's Word.

Prayer

In the name of Jesus, I thank You God my Father because You are very faithful in my life. I have seen and read that You can never abandon me. Father keep helping me to believe and acknowledge this fact in Jesus name I pray, Amen!

Isaiah 43.2 / *When you pass through the waters, I will be with you; and through the rivers, they shall not overwhelm you; when you walk through fire you shall not be burned, and the flame shall not consume you.*

Deuteronomy 31:6 ESV / *Be strong and courageous. Do not fear or be in dread of them, for it is the Lord your God who goes with you. He will not leave you or forsake you."*

Joshua 1:9 ESV / *Have I not commanded you? Be strong and courageous. Do not be frightened, and do not be dismayed, for the Lord your God is with you wherever you go."*

Isaiah 49:15-16 ESV / *"Can a woman forget her nursing child, that she should have no compassion on the son of her womb? Even these may forget, yet I will not forget you. Behold, I have engraved you on the palms of my hands; your walls are continually before me."*

Romans 8:38-39 ESV / *For I am sure that neither death nor life, nor angels nor rulers, nor things present nor things to come, nor powers, nor height nor depth, nor anything else in all creation, will be able to separate us from the love of God in Christ Jesus our Lord.*

THE WAITING GAME REDEFINED

Have you ever been in a situation where you have done your best and performed to the best of your ability? A situation where you have done everything that you can do and where you areat a place of no hope? There are different aspects of waiting. It can be daunting no matter what context you find yourself in. Waiting can be a disheartening task regardless of who you are and what youare waiting for. I don't know about you, but I definitely don't like waiting. Whether it be waiting for a doctor's appointment, waiting in traffic, waiting on that acceptance letter, waiting for school admission, waiting for an interview, waiting to be married, waiting to have a child, or waiting for a callback on an important decision—waiting can be difficult. The waiting period can be one of the most crucial aspects of someone's life because, during this period, you are under pressure to use every power and resource at your disposal to control the situation.

However, your perception during the waiting process is dependent on what you're doing while waiting.

Here are some ways to stay winning and triumph any waiting period in your life.

One

"How?" You may ask. Well, because you are a believer, you have an advantage. In life, we are taught that what you put in, is what you get back. The truth is, as a Christian, a believer of Jesus Christ, you don't just get what you put in; you get more than you put in because you are in Christ and Christ is in God. Don't get me wrong, I am not saying you don't have to put in the work or effort. You should put in more than your best. Notice what I said there? You must put in more than your best because sometimes your best isn't enough. Invite God, by the help of the Holy Spirit, to overshadow you. When you put in more than your best, that is the addition of grace to it. When God is involved, favor is added to it. God's good thoughts are added to it and all these things are working together for you (Romans 8:28). Having this understanding is the key factor in changing how you wait on your breakthrough. Now, imagine knowing all these, and yet you beat yourself up when you are in between answers.

Two

Know what is certain. Familiarize yourself with the things that are certain and completely unchangeable. Like the word of God. "Heaven and Earth will pass but my word NEVER passes away" Matthew 24:35. Get immersed in the word of God and dwell in it continually. Meditate on what God said about you because God's word is the one thing that is certain and can never change. I have learned that as life goes on and seasons change, we can become prisoners of many things like bad thoughts, negative outcomes, bad relationships, bad health, etc. However, there is one thing that we can never go wrong in and that is being a prisoner of hope. As stated in Zechariah \9;12. Being a prisoner of hope means letting only your expectations and beliefs in the abilities of God be the only things that occupy your mind. It means being bound in the hope of God's strength to bring and manifest what you expect and what He has promised you. Dwell on the things that are God's reality of you, "the thoughts I have for you are the thoughts of good and not of evil" (Jeremiah 29:11). The implication of this is knowing that it doesn't matter what the outcome might be, it can never work against you. The outcome can never work against what is CERTAIN which is the word of God over your life.

Three

Intentionally trash negative words and vibes. A vibe is energy. Energy can be transmitted through people, environments, feelings, music, books, etc. You can get energy from almost anything and anyone. When energy or vibes are transmitted to you, they can leave you with an uplifting spirit or with sadness. The anxieties of waiting can cloud your judgment and make you lose sight of the fact that you are in charge. It can derail your thoughts and question everything you know to be true. What comes to you during this period is vital, you must not entertain negative stories of others during your waiting period. The waiting period is not the time to google, "how many MRI results end up as a cancer diagnosis?" It is not the time to look up divorce statistics, or the time to question if you are too old to find the right spouse, or too damaged to be loved. And it is not the time to look up university admission or rejection rates. It is a privileged time of cleansing and detoxing your mind, environment, and people. It is a time of focusing on your desired outcome because whatever you dwell on rubs off on you. If you stay in a house where everyone is smoking when you step out, you will smell like smoke whether you participated in smoking or not. No matter what the feeling is, whether it be hopelessness, temptation depression, anxiety, anger - you name it – it might try to overshadow you. Trash it. You cannot be victorious while dwelling in negativity. Your perspective and mindset can help you remain unclogged from negativity through the help of God. Let God transform you into a new person by changing the way you think. Then you will learn to know God's will for you, which is good, pleasing, and perfect (Romans 12:2 NLT).

Four

Exercise self-control and trust God through this process. The waiting period is not a time of personal gratification. It is not a time of seeking the easiest solution, nor is it a time of looking for a temporary fix. Why? Because when you are frustrated, you don't think rationally. Instead, you find yourself making hasty decisions that could destroy your life. When you lose self-control, your sensitivity gets clouded with frustration, uneasiness, and impatience. It is easy to forget and realize the good things this waiting period can bring you. Self-control is a fruit of the Holy Spirit. Not only is it important but it also brings peace - peace that comes from the knowledge of God's ability. During the waiting period, things seem to take longer than usual, circumstances linger, and the pressure heightens. You often seem to experience different emotions at once whether you are deeply rooted in your faith or not. However, trusting God during this period is crucial. Trust can be very difficult for someone who is used to being in charge, it can be scary and sometimes very unfamiliar.

But the truth is when you trust, when you completely surrender, you experience the strength of God in you. When you give up on your strengths and abilities, then God gives you His strength, His abilities, His grace - which in turn bring you the miracles and the fulfillment you seek. Trusting is not a sign of weakness, neither is it a sign of complacency. Don't let your mind or the voice of the devil, or even any human, stop you from totally trusting God's process.

Although the waiting period can be a time of ambiguity, uncertainty, discouragement, and depression. The perception of God and certainty on His word, on one's self-control, and the right mindset can change how you experience this period. When you know the amount of power that you exert over your mind, you will be more inclined to know how to make every period, including the waiting period, work for you and not against you. I want to encourage you that, with the help of God, you will remain calm and not be quivered or make a mistake during your waiting period. Be wise to set your priorities right so that a misplaced priority doesn't derail your outcome. The waiting period can either be a frustrating period or a period of confidence and calmness depending on how you perceive and handle it. It doesn't have to be frustrating for you. I pray that God's peace, love, and kindness serenades you always and, most especially, during the period of waiting for a breakthrough.

Action Step

Every time you feel overwhelmed during your waiting period, pray and pour out your heart and emotions to God. Ask Him to give you the strength to keep you going. Ask Him to give you sensitivity, and to help you remain faithful, committed, and grateful.

PRAYER FOR SALVATION

Perhaps you are someone who is doubting where you stand with God or someone who desires to go deeper with God. You can give your life to Christ by praying the prayer of Salvation. The prayer of salvation is your acknowledgment of Jesus Christ as Lord and Savior and that makes you born again!

So, if that's you, repeat after me:

Lord Jesus, I recognize the sacrifice that You made on my behalf by your suffering, death, and resurrection which brought about the victory over Satan. Lord I appreciate you. I ask that from today, moving forward, that You come into my life as my Lord and personal Savior. Forgive me of my sins and make me a new being in You. I receive the gift of salvation through Jesus Christ with the help of the Holy Spirit. Amen!

Congratulations on making the important decisions of your life! There are few things you can do now:

1. Grow in your faith and walk with God
2. Connect with people who are believers of Jesus Christ
3. Prayerfully find a Bible believing church and be planted.

www.ingramcontent.com/pod-product-compliance
Lightning Source LLC
LaVergne TN
LVHW050610100826
845148LV00015B/3208

* 9 7 8 1 7 3 6 2 1 8 3 4 1 *